ADAPTED FOR THE ___
READER BY JAMES HARRIS

ISBN: 9798359608060

INTRODUCTION

For many years I have been training Ni Ten Ichi Ryu otherwise called the Way of Strategy, and now for the first time I wish to express it in writing. During the first ten days of the tenth month in the twentieth year of Kanei (1645) I climbed mountain Iwato to pay my respects to heaven above, ^{pray} to the Goddess of mercy, and meditate on the teachings of Buddha. I am a warrior of Musashi now aged sixty.

As a youth my soul drew me to the Way of strategy. I had my first fight at thirteen and beat Arima Kihei a strategist of the Shinto school. At sixteen I defeated Tadashima Akiyama a well esteemed strategist at the time. At twenty-one I journeyed to the capital and challenged all types of strategists, without any failures.

From here I travelled province to province challenging many strategists from countless schools. Around sixty encounters without a loss. All of this was between the ages of thirteen to twenty-nine.

At thirty I began to reflect on my past. The triumphs did not seem to me that I had mastered strategy. It was more like a natural skill, God's will, or the other schools' teachings were inferior. Upon this reflection I decided every morning and evening to study the greatest principles, and at the age of fifty I fully understood the Way of strategy.

From that point, I have been living without following any specific Way. I practise many arts and skills, without a teacher.

To write this book I did invoke Buddha's laws or the teachings of Confucius, I did not reference historic war or books on martial arts. I write to explain the true soul of the Way, which is also mirrored in the Way of heaven and Buddhism. It is currently the tenth day of the tenth month, 3am.

STRATEGY

Strategy is the expertise of a warrior. Leaders must understand and action this craft, and soldiers should also understand it. Yet at the time of writing this, there appears to be no warrior in the world that really understands strategy.

There are various systems for people to follow. The Way of Salvation through the law of Buddha, the Way of education through the works of Confucius, the Way of healing as a doctor, or the Way of Art, through tea ceremony and archery, along with many other practicable skills. Each man should practice that which he feels inclined to.

It can be said the Way of a warrior is twofold, it consists of the pen and sword, and he should have an appetite for both. If a man lacks natural capability, he can still be a warrior by training diligently both aspects of the Way.

Generally speaking, the warrior's Way is a firm acceptance of death. Although this is not only reserved for warriors, but women, peasants and priests, are known to have died during the course of duty, but that is a different matter.

The Way of strategy as studied by warriors is based on defeating other men. Victory is won by engaging in combat with individuals, or commanding large numbers during conflict. By doing so we can achieve power and notoriety for ourselves or for our lord. These are the advantages of strategy.

THE WAY OF STRATEGY

In Japan and China those that practice the Way are known to be "masters of strategy". All true warriors learn the Way.

Lately, there have been some roaming the world claiming to be strategists, but they are nothing but simple sword-fencers. Those that attended the Kashima Kantori shrines in the province of Hitachi believed they received direct instruction from the gods, and made these teachings based on this. They now travel from country to country instructing men on how to sword fight. This is the current prevalent meaning of strategy.

In times of the past, strategy was recommended as one of the Ten Abilities and Seven Arts to be cultivated as a valuable practice. It most certainly was an art, but its value as a practice was not limited to sword-fighting. The true value of sword-fighting will not be seen when focusing on sword-fencing technique. Outside of this limited scope the value is to be found. It is what it can do for you, not: what it is.

When we take a look around, we see various arts for sale. As an extension men use equipment to sell a part of themselves. Similar to the acorn and the oak, as if the acorn has become less than the oak. In this Way of strategy, both the teacher and the student are concerned with showing off their skill, trying to forcefully rush the growth of their oak. The student speaks of their Dojo. The teacher is looking for profit.

It was once said "Undeveloped strategy is the cause of misery". Truth can be found in this saying.

There are four Ways in which men can travel along the road of life: as a farmer, as a merchant, a warrior or artisan.

The Way of the farmer: oversees spring to autumn, with a keen eye on seasonal changes. Utilises agricultural tools to turn invisible into visible, supporting growth through meticulous nourishment and care.

The Second Way is that of the merchant: Through a combination of ingredients the wine maker cultivates his product and makes his living through sales. The Way of the merchant is to calculate his costs and add a markup to his products thus being able to live from profit.

Thirdly the Way of the warrior: a warrior carries the weaponry of his Way and he masters the virtue of his weapons. If a warrior disregards strategy he will not appreciate the benefit of his weaponry, so he must have an appetite for strategy

Fourthly the Way of the artisan. An artisan becomes proficient in the use of his tools, lays his plans with an accurate measure and then carries out his work according to the plan. For example, a carpenter always measures twice and cuts once.

These are the four Ways of the farmer, merchant, warrior and the artisan.

Why compare the Way of the artisan to a Carpenter? The comparison with carpentry is through the connection to houses. Houses of aristocrats, houses of warriors. The carpenter uses the architectural plans of the building, and the Way of strategy here, is similar in that there is a plan of attack. Just as, if you want to learn the strategy of war, continue reading this book. The teacher is a needle, the student is the thread. You must give constant practice.

Like a carpenter, the commander must know the fundamental rules, then the rules of the country, and the rules of home. This is the Way of the commander.

The carpenter must know architectural theories of construction, not only houses but also the development of palaces, and must be able to direct men to create either according to the plan. The Way of the carpenter is the same as the Way of the commander of a house of warriors.

When constructing houses, various types of wood may be used. Very straight unknotted timber is used for interior pillars, while straight timber without defects is used for the more visible areas of the household such as thresholds and doors. The strongest timber even if it defective in appearance can be used discreetly in construction. The weakest of timber should only be use for scaffolding and then burnt as firewood.

The master carpenter distributes the workload for his men each according to their ability. Flooring specialists, door makers, thresholds and ceiling fitters etc. Beginners lay floor joists, and those of even less ability cut wood other miscellaneous work like clearing the site. If master carpenter knows the skills of his men and distributes the work correctly the finished product will be of high standard.

The master carpenter has to take into account the skills and limits of his workers, and ask nothing unreasonable of them. He must understand their spirit, boost their morale and encourage them when it is necessary. This is the same as the principle of strategy.

A carpenter sharpens his own tools, as a soldier maintains his weapons. He works under the direction of the master carpenter, he lays flooring, fits kitchen units, installs doors, and carves woodwork with a smooth finish.

This is a carpenter's art, and once his skills are perfected, and he understands measurements accurately, he can become a master carpenter. However, all the elements that make a master carpenter must be mastered first, one cannot be omitted. It is very much the same for a warrior, think deeply about this.

High skills of a carpenter are that his joints line perfectly, and that his woodwork is not warped and appears to merge seamlessly so that it does not look like segregated pieces stuck together. This is essential.

If you want to understand and learn the Way, you must contemplate what is written and think deeply about it.

THE FIVE BOOKS OF THE WAY

The Way is laid out in the following five books (rings):

1. Ground
2. Water
3. Fire
4. Wind
5. Void

Consider the Ground book as a road map along the ground, wherever we step, this is always the base. The ground must be secure, for us to walk without risk of falling.

The water book seeks to mould the spirit to become like water. Filling the shape of wherever it goes, water can be still, trickle, or crash hard. Water can be clear, or clouded.

The book of Fire is about developing a fighting spirit. Fire is intense regardless of whether it is small or large; and it is the same with one-on-one combat, or armies at war.

There must be an appreciation for the fighting spirit.

The Wind book, discusses old traditions, new traditions, and the thinking of friends and family which differs from the Way. Because you cannot know yourself, if you do not know others.

Finally, the book of the Void. That with no end and no beginning. Achieving this means not achieving this. The Way of strategy is the Way of nature. When you can fully appreciate the power of nature, and see its rhythms to be found in any situation, you will be able to strike naturally and defeat any enemy.

THE GROUND BOOK

This book lays the groundwork.

Ichi Ryu Ni To means: One school two swords.

Warriors carry two swords with them. The long sword and the sword. There is an advantage to using two weapons. There is also the spear and the axe.

Students of the Way of strategy should initially start training with the sword and long sword in both hands. The truth is, if you face potentially losing your life you must make full use of your weaponry, what a disgrace it would be to die with your weapons undrawn.

Do not hold a sword with two hands, as it is difficult to wield it left and right. Instead hold it in one hand only.

When riding a horse through various terrain or through crowds of people, it is difficult to carry a sword in both hands. Holding a long sword in both hands is not the correct Way, however when there is difficulty slicing an enemy, you must use both hands. To use a sword in one hand is not difficult. Train with two, one in each hand. At first it will seem difficult, but it will eventually get easier. Which is the case with all new training. Train with a bow, and your pull becomes stronger. When you are accustomed to sword your power will increase, and you will understand the Way.

There is no quick method to be able to master the long sword. As it is long, it is meant to be used in large motions which get smaller over time, and the smaller sword in small motions which get larger over time. This is the first thing to understand.

The teaching, however, of the Ichi school, is to understand that one can win with the long as well as the short weapon, what is primarily taught at Ichi, is the spirit of winning regardless of the weapon or size.

When facing multiple enemies, it's better to use two swords rather than one. Even more so, if you wish to capture at least one of them.

Some things cannot be explained in

detail, yet knowing one thing, can mean knowing ten thousand things. Therefore, when you grasp the Way of strategy nothing else will be invisible.

Study hard!

THE BENEFIT OF TWO DIFFERENT TYPES OF PEOPLE READING STRATEGY

We call long sword masters, strategists. Those with the bow are called archers, with the spear are called spearmen, and with the gun are called marksmen. However, we do not call those with the long sword "long swordsmen". Because bows, spears and guns are all warriors' equipment and definitely form part of strategy. To master the long sword makes one able to master himself and his world, therefore the longsword forms the basis of strategy. One man can beat ten others if he masters the long sword. And if one man can beat ten, one hundred can beat a thousand, and a thousand can beat ten thousand. Yet, my strategy makes one equal to ten thousand, making it the complete warrior's craft.

The warrior's Way does not in include other Ways, such as: Taoism, Buddhism, or any particular tradition, artistic craft or dance. But by following the warrior's Way, you will begin to see it more broadly in everything. Each man must perfect their particular Way.

THE BENEFIT OF WEAPONS IN STRATEGY

All weapons have their time and place. The small sword is best used in a confined space, or when engaged in close combat. The spear is useful at long distance. The spear is essentially a field weapon and not suitable for taking a prisoner. However, the long sword is beneficial in all situations.

Mastering indoor techniques while neglecting the outdoors, teaches one to think narrowly, and forget the true Way. You will then have difficulty in real life situations.

A bow is a strong weapon of choice at the beginning of a battle, as it is possible to take aim and fire quickly from a distance. However, in close range altercations it is effectively useless. Therefore, there are no longer many schools teaching archery.

The handgun has replaced the bow, however one of the most useful aspects of firing a bow, is that one can see the trajectory and their flight path, and correct the aim as necessary. With a handgun, the shots are not visible, there must be some appreciation for this aspect of the bow and the importance of this.

As a horse must have endurance and no defects, so should be the case with weapons. Made to last and are there for heavy use not decoration.

Do not have a favourite type of weapon, one which you become accustomed to and prefer. Familiarity of one weapon over others is a fault just as it is not to know how to use it. Do not copy others, use the weapons which you can handle correctly. It is a detriment for commanders to have preferences. These things you must acknowledge and learn thoroughly.

TIMING IN STRATEGY

Timing is in everything, and timing in strategy can only be learnt with a great deal of practice. Timing is found in music and dance, and rhythm overlays timing, and it is so, that timing and rhythm are also found in the military arts of attacking and defending. In all skills and abilities there is timing.

TIMING THE VOID

Timing is found in the life of the warrior, his strength and weakness, his peak and his decline. Similar to the timing of a business man, and the rise and fall of his capital. In strategy you must be aware of various timing considerations. From the very start you must know the timing applicable and that which is not, and in all things large or small find the relevant timing. It is at the height of importance that you know the background timing, and determine your enemy's timing, then subsequently using a timing the enemy does not expect.

Each of the five books are connected to timing. You must train rigorously in timing to appreciate it's importance.

If you train daily in this Ichi school strategy, your spirit will broaden naturally. Common principles in each book are laid out here for all men who want to learn my strategy:

♦ **Do not act or think dishonestly.**

♦ **The Way can be found in training.**

♦ **Train and know the Way in all arts.**

♦ **Know the difference between gain and loss in all matters.**

♦ **Develop intuition and clear judgement.**

♦ **Understand that which**

cannot be seen.

♦ **Pay attention to the smallest of details.**

♦ **Do nothing without use or purpose.**

Start by inscribing these broad principles in your heart, and begin to train in the Way of strategy. If you cannot understand the overview, it will be difficult for you to master strategy in the details. If you learn and attain this strategy you will never lose to a single enemy. Most importantly, from now you must set your heart on mastering strategy and solemnly stick to the Way. On this path, you will find yourself beating men in fights, and also able to win with just your eyes. Moreover, by training your body will become free, it will be under your control, and you will beat men with it, however with sufficient training you will be able to beat ten men with your spirit alone. At this point, will it not mean that you are invincible?

Also, during large scale strategy offensives the superior man will be able to manage many subordinates with ease, carry himself correctly, run the country and assist the people, consequently preserving the ruler's discipline. If there is a Way of the indomitable spirit, self-help and to gain honour, it is the Way of strategy.

The second year of Shoho (1645), the fifth month, the twelfth day.

Teruo   Magonojo"   SHINMEN MUSASHI.

THE WATER BOOK

The spirit of the strategy is based on water. This Book teaches the long sword form and methods of victory. Language finds difficulty explaining the Way in detail, but intuitively it can be understood. Take time with this book, contemplate each word, if you fail to grasp it, the Way will be lost.

The principles of strategy will be laid out for one-on-one combat, but thinking more broadly you will be able to apply them to battles with a vast number of troops.

Any deviation from the Way of Strategy could be catastrophic.

Do not simply read these words, this will not lead you to fully understand the Way of Strategy. As well, do not simply remember and apply what you learn, you must fill your heard and your body with the Way.

SPIRITUAL BEARING IN STRATEGY

When applying strategy your spiritual bearing must be the same as when you are at rest. In battle and standard civilian life, you must be both indomitable yet composed. The situation requires a state of relaxation but not thoughtlessly, your spirit unruffled yet neutral.

When the spirit is at rest the body is awake, and when your body is awake do not let the spirit sleep. Your spirit therefore should not be affected by your body, and your body not affected by your spirit.

Do not be of weak spirit, or an over enthusiastic spirit. A highly active spirit is feeble and a lifeless spirit is frail. The enemy should not see your spirit.

Smaller people have to become acquainted with the spirit of larger people., and larger people have to become aware of a small person's spirit.

Regardless of your own size, do not be fooled by the responses of your body.

With an open spirit, take a bird's eye

view.

Develop your wisdom, intuition and spirit. Understand justice, recognise good and evil. Study the Ways of other arts one at a time.

When a man can no longer deceive you, you have developed the wisdom of strategy.

You should continually study the principles of strategy so that you can develop a composed spirit.

STANCE IN STRATEGY

Keep the head up as if suspended on a string from the crown, do not let it hang down, or fix it looking up, and definitely not twisted.

The forehead should not be frowning, and skin between your eyes should not squeeze inward. No wrinkles. Do not let the eyes dart from side to side, or blink, but them let them rest as if falling asleep.

No with your face composed, keep the nose facing directly forward, and the nostrils slightly flared.

The rear of the neck should be straight: feel energy rush to your hair and all the Way from the shoulders down through your entire body. Let the shoulders drop, put power into your legs from the tops, up through the knees, and buttocks so that the buttocks do not stick out. Tense the abdomen so your hips do not rotate forward.

Maintain this battle stance at all times. Your everyday stance should be no different.

GAZE IN STRATEGY

Vision must be wide-ranging for two purposes, to perceive and to see. Perception is stronger than seeing.

It is of great importance to see what is distant as if it were close, and that which is close as if it were far away. It is essential to observe the enemy's weaponry, yet to know to be distracted by insignificant movements of it. Your vision should be the same for single combat as well as large scale conflict.

You must be able to see left and right

without moving the eyeballs. Mastering this ability is a slow process and will take time. Practise this gaze every day, in general life and do not use any other form of observing.

HOLDING THE LONG SWORD

The sword must be held by the thumb and forefinger in a manner which feels light; the middle finger not tight nor loose, and the last two fingers should have a tight grip.

Hold the sword with an intention on cutting your enemy, and as you cut through him, do not change the grip.

The flexibility and looseness of the thumb and forefinger come in to play when defending or pushing the enemy's sword to one side. General I loathe immobility in the hands and in life. That which is fixed is dead, and that which moves has life. Keep this in mind.

FOOTWORK

The toes should glide, yet the heels are

firm on the ground. In fast and slow movements always move naturally. This is the Yin-Yang foot, which is of importance to the Way. But this does not mean the use of only one foot. You must move from left to the right, and right to the left, when cutting, or defending. There should be no preferential foot.

THE FIVE STYLES

There are five styles to adopt: up, down, central, left or right. Each is a method to cut, and which ever attitude you are in, do not be conscious of the style, focus on the cutting.

Your movement should be large or small depending on the situation. Up, down and central are decisive, while left and right are fluid. Left and right are to be used when obstructions are overhead, or on either side. This depends on location.

To grasp the Way and to understand style it is necessary to know the centre. The central style is the heart of the five styles.

When looking at strategy broadly, the central style is the commander, and the other four follow the orders of the central command.

THE WAY OF THE LONG SWORD

When one knows the Way of the long sword, they will be able to handle it with as little as two fingers. Knowing the path of this sword well, makes its use effortless.

Try to use the long sword too quickly and you will lose the Way. To be able to handle the long sword well one must be able to use it calmly. If you try to move it rapidly like the short sword, with quick thrusts, you will make mistakes, as you cannot cut a man using the long sword in this manner.

When cutting, return the sword along the same path, to cut downward means raising the sword upward to return, cut left or right means a sideways return in the opposing direction. Have the elbows wide, and wield the sword strongly.

To be proficient in the long sword you must learn the five approaches and train them constantly.

THE FIVE APPROACHES

- The primary approach is the central style. Attack your enemy with the sword directly toward the face. When he responds, deflect his sword to the left or right, or downward. Let your sword remain where it is and as he attempts to attack again cut his arm off.

You must train constantly to master the long sword, and then I assure you, you will be able to control any enemy attack. There are no further styles that these I present to you.

- The secondary approach of the long sword is to engage from the upper style and cut the enemy in the same moment as his attack. If he evades you, do not move the blade, then return to the upper position from below and cut him as he launches his next attack.

Timing and spirit changes are required. You will be able to learn these by training in the Ichi school. You cannot lose when you have learnt the five approaches, but you must train repeatedly to master them all.

- The third approach is to position oneself in the lower style, ready to swipe upward. When the enemy makes his move, cut his hands off from below. If he tries to deflect your sword downward, cut his arm off horizontally while feeling yourself crossing from left to right or right to left. Strike the enemy in the same moment as his attack.

This is a common method which you will use as a beginner and later on in your development. You must train to hold the sword well.

- The fourth approach is to position to the left. As the enemy makes his attack, slash the hands of from the side. If he attempts to deflect your sword, parry his sword in the same direction and then cut across from the shoulder.

With this method you will learn to parry the sword into the enemy's line of attack. Study this well.

- The fifth approach is to step to the right and as the enemy attacks, swing the sword across and cut the arm off.

This method is essential in learning to hold the long sword well and moving it with strength.

This is a mere description of the approaches, yet as with all the teachings in this book, you must practice to fully know the Way. You will always win with these five approaches if you also consider the enemy's spirit and timing.

THE TEACHING OF 'STYLE AND NO STYLE'

The title above means that means that as well as knowing the five styles one must also consider holding no style at all.

Although there only five styles, you must hold the sword in whichever Way is best to cut the enemy, and this relates to the location and the enemy's stance. The upper style can morph into the middle style, and then to the lower and back up to the upper style. The point to note is that there is not only one style and that you must not hold one style without the flexibility to move to another.

The main intention of cutting the enemy remains the same, whenever you strike or parry, you should also cut the enemy whilst doing so. It is vital to understand this.

If you only think of parrying, or defending, you will not cut him. Your movement must have the intention of cutting.

Battle Array is another topic for

winning large scale wars. Again no one style will do, a fixed formation is bad. Study this well.

STRIKE THE ENEMY "IN THE MOMENT OF VOID"

The moment of void means when the enemy appears indecisive, in this moment is when you must strike rapidly without moving your body.

You must train well to recognise, and achieve the timing required to strike in this moment.

TWO TIMING

Attack the enemy and as he defends observe him tense up, and then as he relaxes follow up and cut him.

Again, it is difficult to comprehend this only by reading this book, one must experience to fully understand.

SPIRIT FIRE

When the enemy attacks, and you decide the timing is right to counter attack, strike with your body, hit hard with your spirit, and powerfully with your hands.

This is the most often used style of striking. You have to train to fully understand it.

FLOW LIKE WATER

If at all you struggle against an enemy, when he withdraws to launch a strike, enlarge your body and spirit and cut him slowly with the long sword.

CONTINUOUS CUTTING

In one continuous motion cut the head arms and legs off. Cutting several places in one is called the continuous cut. one action cut his head, hands and legs. This technique is used often, with much practice you will grasp it.

FIRE AND STONES

Cut the enemy with the power of the legs, torso and hands, all at the same time without raising the sword. Train this technique well and you will strike powerfully.

RED LEAVES

With the fire and stones technique above strike the tip of the enemy's sword down and watch it drop from his hands, just like the red leaves that fall from a tree.

THE BODY

The body and sword usually move in unison; however, you can strike with the body then the sword, but if the enemy is immovable, you can also strike with the sword then the body.

CUT AND SLICE

Cutting and slicing are not the same. Cutting is a decision with a strong spirit, while slicing is merely touching the enemy's skin. You must distinguish this suitable difference. Learn this well.

MONKEY'S BODY

The notion here is that the body of a monkey is used and not the arms. It is to get close with the body within arm's reach. Understand distance and research this well.

BODY GLUE

Stick to the enemy and do not allow separation. Some only use the hands and legs and tend to keep the body at a distance. With this technique one clings firm without a degree of separation to the enemy's body. Consider this.

REACH FOR HEIGHT

Stretch the legs hips and neck to be as tall as possible, bit also be higher in thinking and attitude. When you think you have won, and believe your height is superior strike powerfully. Learn this.

BE STICKY

When the enemy strikes allow your sword to stick to his. Feel the motion and direction, stick to it and follow it until you finally control the direction. This is not a spirit of striking, it is one of maintaining contact. There is also a difference between sticking and being entangled. Sticking is the choice of contact, while entanglement is a feeling of needing to escape (which is weak). Know this difference.

BODY STRIKES

A body strike is made by finding a gap in the enemy's guard. Turn your face to the side, but keep the eyes on the enemy, then thrust with the shoulder straight in to the chest forcefully. By doing so, you can knock your enemy up to twenty feet away or until he is dead. Train this well.

THREE WAYS TO PARRY

1. Smack the enemy's sword to the side as if aiming for one of his eyes.
2. Rebound his sword towards one of his eyes as if intending to slice his neck.
3. While holding a short sword along with the long sword, close in quickly, and thrust the short sword in his face.

Bear in mind that you can always clench your hand around your sword so as to make a fist, and punch at the enemy's face. Train well.

STAB AT THE FACE

Maintain an intention to stab the face. Trace your line of sight along the edge of the blade with the tip directed at the face. When the enemy's body ducks you have an opportunity to end the duel by trampling on him and slicing him up. So, make sure to train this technique well.

STAB AT THE HEART

When there is restricted space for attack, stab at the enemy's chest without letting the long sword slacken at all. This technique is also useful if we have fatigued or the blade is no longer sharp and able to cut.

SCOLD

Scold the enemy, when he attempts his counter cut, you counter cut again teaching him a lesson. This is a matter of impeccable timing. You will only grasp this with repetitive practice.

SMACKING PARRY

The essence of the smacking parry is not to smack hard, but rather to co-ordinate with great timing the exact force of the enemy so as to simply let the swords clash and bounce off each other. If you hold this skill, your sword will never be knocked from your hand. Practise well.

MANY ENEMIES

This technique applies if you are outnumbered. Draw both swords and stretch out as wide as possible. Chase the enemies around even if they attack from all sides. Notice the order of attack, and respond to whoever attacks first.

The order of their attacks is most important to note. Swipe left and right, right and left alternatively. Do not wait, this is dangerous, maintain your attack. Control the dynamic. Bring the enemy together as if stringing a line of fish, and once drawn together, cut them all down forcefully without allowing any room for movement and without mercy.

THE ADVANTAGE OF FIGHTING

You can know how to win with the strategy of fighting, but you cannot win without practising it. The win cannot be explained in writing, only through practise can it be fully understood. The true Way of strategy is revealed through putting in to practise what is learnt.

ONE CUT

The spirit of one cut allows for a definite win. However, obtaining this spirit without practise does not ensue. If you train diligently the Way of strategy will be engrained in your heart.

DIRECT COMMUNICATION

Direct Communication is the method by which the Way of the Ichi school is revealed and passed down. The oral tradition generally asks that one teaches their body strategy."

The book above is an outline of the teachings of the Ichi school in regards to sword fighting.

Absorb the contents, focusing on one part at a time, and then with practise you will slowly come to recognise the Way.

A thousand-mile road is travelled step

by step. So, diligently study strategy and over the years to come you will acquire the warrior's spirit. Today conquer yourself, and tomorrow you will conquer weaker men. Then, to conquer stronger and more skilful men, continue to follow the teachings in this book and do not let your heart be discouraged or taken off track. Even if you are victorious over a man, if this was not won through the teachings found in this book, it is not the True Way.

If you attain victory by following the Way, assuredly you will be able to triumph over thousands of men.

On this twelfth day, the fifth month, the second year of Shoho, (1645) MUSASHI.

THE FIRE BOOK

This Book of Fire belonging to the Ichi school describes fighting as fire.

Some do not perceive the benefit in strategy and think narrowly. As if they are only aware of their arms and not the dexterity of the finger tips and therefore do not appreciate the full advantage of strategy.

My teachings are for killing enemies, and the full education is only developed by contest, fighting to save one's own life, learning the Way of the sword, estimating the strength of an attack and delivering the appropriate response. The true Way of strategy is a guaranteed method for winning one on one, or against ten. One man can beat ten, and a thousand can beat ten thousand.

It is not practical to assemble a thousand men for daily training, but individually you can become a master of strategy by training alone, so you can understand the enemy's strategies, and strength, and develop counter strategy to defeat anyone.

Any man who desires to master strategy must train morning and evening. By doing so he can refine his skill, become free from the self, and develop an astonishing ability. He will hold immense power. This is the very real result of strategy.

THE PLACE

Examine your environment, and keep the sun behind you. If this is not possible, aim to keep the sun on your right side. Indoors, keep the entrance behind you, your rear must be unobstructed, and you must have free space on either side. At night, keep the fire behind you to be able to see the enemy clearly. Look down upon the enemy as if standing on an exalted plane.

When the fight begins, chase and drive the enemy to the left side. Press him towards the most awkward of places, and try to keep his back to the wall. When the enemy is found in a troublesome position, do not give him any chance to look around to find his escape, thoroughly pin him down further.

In houses, drive the enemy toward the doors and pillars, again not letting him see his surroundings.

Always pressure the enemy toward awkward places, with obstacles at his sides, using the features of the place to establish dominant positions from which to fight. This must be trained well.

THREE METHODS TO FORESTALL THE ENEMY

1. To set him up: Ken No Sen.
2. To wait for the advantage: Tai No Sen.
3. To accompany him: Tai-Tai No Sen.

THE FIRST: KEN NO SEN

When you have decided to make an attack, move in quickly but keep a calm spirit. The calm and reserved spirit will forestall him.

Alternately, move forward with a powerful spirit but move your feet faster than usual, ultimately disturbing him.

Or, with a calm spirit, attack heavily with the thought totally crushing the enemy's spirit right down to the depths of his being.

THE SECOND: TAI NO SEN

When the enemy makes an attack, stay as calm as possible but act as if you becoming weak. As the enemy believes his moment has come to crush you, move rapidly and suddenly, jump to the side, and attack powerfully as soon as you notice the enemy relax.

Or, when the enemy attacks, counter-attack with a stronger force, take advantage of any timing errors to win.

THE THIRD: TAI-TAI NO SEN

When the enemy makes an attack, you must attack with a calm spirit but powerfully. Aim for his weaknesses and win.

Or, as the enemy attacks calmly, observe his movements and, move with him as if floating on a cloud. Then suddenly move quickly and cut him.

These things are not able to be fully described with words, you must practise and experience these to understand. Forestalling means that one does now always make the first move, but by forestalling you have essentially won, so you must train this well.

<u>HOLDING A PILLOW DOWN</u>

Do not allow the opponents head to rise, essentially holding it down like a pillow.

When fighting it is bad to allow the opponent to lead you. You must be able to lead the enemy. The enemy will no doubt also have this in mind, but he cannot forestall you if you do not allow him to rise. While fighting; as he attempts to cut, you must push his sword downward, and when he tries to grapple you must throw him off and down. This is the meaning of "holding a pillow down". When you have understood this principle, it does not matter what the enemy attempts as you will perceive it early and crush it. Your spirit will be able block an attack before the word begins, when he tries to jump, he will be knocked down at "ju…", and his cut blocked at "cu . . .".

It is important in strategy to suppress the enemy's useful attacks but let his blunders play out. However, if you do this only, you are being purely defensive, and to follow the true Way, you must lead the enemy. When you can do this, you will be a master of strategy. You must train constantly and understand the method of "holding a pillow down".

CROSSING AT A FORD

Crossing at a ford, means, for example, crossing the sea, or a river, a marsh or harsh terrain. I believe the time comes many times in every man's life to cross. It could mean sailing away while your acquaintances remain in the harbour, choosing your own route, and knowing if your ship is ready for the journey. With all conditions met, and a favourable wind behind you, set sail. If the wind changes before you arrive at the destination, row the remaining miles without a sail.

This spirit applies to everyday life as it equally does to strategy.

In strategy this means to understand the enemy's weaknesses and your own strengths in comparison, and then cross between them at the most appropriate point. If you succeed and notice the best point, you will cross with ease. This spirit is necessary in small, and in large scale strategy. Research this well.

KNOW THE TIMING

Understanding timing is crucial. Monitor the enemy's energy, is it strong or starting to get loose. By doing so you will be able to take the best position possible and attack accordingly. This principle of strategy allows to an easy win.

When fighting you must stall the enemy until you have determined his energy, his strengths and weaknesses and then you can attack when the moment is ripe.

Determine his reach, and use unsuspected attacks, at the appropriate timing.

Understand timing and you can see right into things. With this strategy, you will easily recognise the enemy's intended actions and therefore have more opportunities to gain victory. Study this well.

<u>TREAD DOWN THE SWORD</u>

This strategy is used when our weapons are ineffective, for example the blade had broken, a rapid move has to be made toward the enemy as fast as possible with the body before he has time to react and even while he raises his sword. This is treading down the sword. To close the gap so that the enemy is unable to use his weapon. The spirit here is to receive the enemy's attack while moving forward for the win.

The enemy must be defeated at the start of his attack, as if trampling him with our feet, so that he cannot rise to the attack further.

By treading I do not literally mean with the feet, I mean with the body and spirit, and where possible the sword. Your spirit must be so strong the enemy will not be able to attack a second time. Study this deeply.

COLLAPSE

It is possible for anything to collapse: a house, a body, an enemy. When fighting, and the enemy is beginning to collapse, do not let the opportunity go to waste, pursue him until he is finished. If you miss this chance, the enemy may recover.

At this moment, you must attack as if chasing the enemy relentlessly so that he cannot recover at all.

BE THE ENEMY

When we allow ourselves to become the enemy, we understand their position. For example, to us a thief in someone else's house is someone that needs to be imprisoned, yet the thief is a mere peasant and to him the man who enters to arrest him is the real hawk. You must appreciate the enemy's position.

In strategy, people generally assume an enemy to be powerful, and this creates caution. Yet, if you have a strong army, and understand strategy properly, you know there is nothing to worry about.

In a combat situation put yourself in the enemy's shoes, but if you were to think 'here is the master of strategy', you will, with no doubt, lose. Contemplate this.

RELEASE FOUR HANDS

The four hands spirit occurs when your hands, and the enemy's hands appear equal. As soon as this is detected you must adopt a different strategy and surprise the enemy.

You must be able to detect this situation immediately.

MOVE THE SHADE

When unable to detect the enemy's position, his spirit remains in the shade to us, we have to prepare a large-scale attack in order to reveal his resources. When you have then determined his strength, use a different strategy to defeat him. Research this well.

HOLDING DOWN A SHADOW

This strategy is used when you are able to detect the enemy's position.

When the enemy makes his attack and you suppress his technique, he will be embarrassed, and this will cause him to change his mind.

TO PASS ON

Many things can be passed on, even a yawn is contagious. Time can also be passed on.

When the enemy is in a rage and rushes for the attack, display the calmest attitude possible, and allow this spirit to be passed on. Watch the enemy become calm and relaxed and then attack suddenly.

You can also infect the enemy with various states such as a carefree, bored or weak spirit. Study this well.

CREATE IMBALANCE

It is important in strategy to create imbalance. Attack when it is unsuspected and defeat him swiftly.

Display a slow and relaxed attitude, then suddenly attack powerfully. Allow no space for recovery, and then take advantage to win. Train this well.

FRIGHTEN

Freight is caused by unexpected situations, you can easily frighten the enemy without the use of force, for example by making the loudest shouting ever, this makes a small situation seem suddenly much worse. Research this technique well.

TO SOAK

When you are in a grapple with the enemy, and you find yourself not able to progress, you soak in and become one with the enemy. Then when the time is right you will find the moment to attack. It is important to understand when to use this method, as in some cases, should you withdraw instead of soaking in, you will lose. Study this well.

INJURE THE CORNERS

In some cases, you will be facing an extremely strong opponent who you cannot defeat head on, you must injure the corners. That means to strike at weak points of the body until he collapses. Once the corners are weakened so to speak, you can then attack directly. Research this well.

THROW IN TO CONFUSION

In large scale war, we use our soldiers to confuse the enemy, by having him guessing, where? Here? There? Now or later? Once confused, victory is guaranteed.

In a one-on-one fight, confusion is created by throw false jabs, feigning a strike, foot work to confuse direction of the attack, and once confused, you can win easily.

THE THREE SHOUTS

There are three times to shout: before, during and after the fight. The voice is energy and conveys life itself.

At the beginning of a battle, shout at loudly as possible. During the fight, shout for each attack. After the fight, shout in victory. These are the three shouts.

During a one-on-one duel, we shout while drawing the short sword, so as to scare and confuse the enemy, and the cut with the long sword. After the enemy is killed, we shout in victory. This is called "sen go no koe" (the before and after voice). We never shout while brandishing the long sword. Research this well.

TO MINGLE

In large scale war, attack the enemy's strongest point until it is weakened, then move on the periphery and attack the next strongest point, like walking a winding path, attack, with draw, attack withdraw.

In a confrontation of one man against multiple attackers, strike the strongest first, then move on to the next. Keep close attention to the enemies' disposition, and show no sign of retreat within your spirit.

In one-on-one combat, use this spirit against the enemy's strongest points one by one.

To mingle, means engaging fully with the enemy, and not retreating at all. Understand this.

TO CRUSH

When the enemy is weak, crush him totally.

In full scale war, when we establish that the enemy is weakened, or has only a few men remaining, knock his head off. That means to say, crush him entirely. If you leave this situation as it is, he may recover. You must develop the spirit to crush without mercy.

In one-on-one combat, if the enemy lacks skill and appears to be evasive, scared, and displaying a retreating attitude, we must crush him immediately, full force, with no other concern, and no space to breath.

Crush entirely, rapidly and do not allow any time or space to recover. You must understand this.

THE MOUNTAIN SEA CHANGE

It is unwise to repeat the same attack more than one time if it did not work the first time. Trying again is unlikely to yield a different result. So, the "mountain-sea" spirit means a change of spirit, as an analogy: to go from the mountain to the sea.

Make the enemy think of the mountain and attack like the sea, and if he thinks of the sea, attack like the mountain. Research this well.

TO PENETRATE THE DEPTHS

In combat, knowing we can win is not enough. If we fail to penetrate the depths, we have only won superficially. To win externally without crushing the opponent's spirit internally is not enough. He may remain undefeated inside and return in the future.

You must train to crush the enemy internally and to the depths of his soul.

TO RENEW

Renewing simply means when we have reached deadlock with the opponent, or have become entangled, that we now disengage, detach and refresh our spirit with a new approach.

It is necessary to understand how to renew in combat. Research this well.

RAT'S HEAD, OX'S NECK

When engaged in combat, we must remember the small details are like the Rat's head and large details like an ox's neck. Whenever we are too interested in the small details we must switch the rat's head for the ox's neck, and then begin to view the larger picture. When we are stuck with only a broad overview, we must switch the ox's neck for the rat's head, and start to understand how the smaller details fit within a larger frame.

This is a necessary spirit for combat and everyday life. Train well.

THE COMMANDER KNOWS THE TROOPS

The commander uses the wisdom of strategy and understands that everyone is under his command, even the enemy. The enemy is one of his troops, and by thinking in this Way, he moves him around like one of his own. Master this.

THE BODY OF A ROCK

Once the Way of strategy has been mastered, you will then be able to turn your body in to a rock. You cannot be broken and nothing can touch you. This is the body of a rock and it cannot be moved.

That which has been recorded above

are my personal thoughts in regards to sword fighting and more broadly, combat in general. Never before have I written about my techniques. I have written it as it came to me and because of that the structure of this book may not be well organised. All that is noted is challenging to express clearly.

This book should be considered as a spiritual guide for the man who wishes to learn the Way of strategy.

From youth my heart has been inclined to the Way of strategy, and I have devoted my life to training, strengthening my body, and developing the various styles, attitudes and spirit.

While watching men of other schools that concentrate on the hand skills only, I have observed that they do not have the true spirit in the slightest.

The men of these schools believe they are training their body and spirit simultaneously, but in reality, they are training the body only, and are not following the true Way of strategy. Their poor influence means that the Way is becoming obscure and dying out.

The true Way of strategy is that of defeating the enemy physically and spiritually, and nothing more than this

If you study and develop the wisdom of my strategy, you will have no doubts about your ability to win.

The second year of Shoho, the fifth month, the twelfth day (1645) Teruo Magonojo SHINMEN MUSASHI

THE WIND BOOK

For comprehensive strategy it is important to observe the Ways of other schools. So, this book of Wind is dedicated to the traditions of those. Without presenting a backdrop my school of Ichi would be harder to understand. My observations of other schools have led me to notice that some focus on strength training, by using longer swords, whilst some specialise in the Way of the short sword known as Kodachi, other schools utilise many techniques of sword use, and teach styles called "surface" and called the Way "interior".

In this book I will lay out why none of these represent the true Way, their virtues, their vices, and also why my school is different. Some of these schools appear to be focused more on ceremony, such as growing decorative flowers and offering awards for good practice, this is certainly not the Way of strategy.

A number of these schools are concerned only with strengthening the body and some skill in use of the sword. But this alone is not sufficient to guarantee a win. This is not the path of the Way.

I will note other school's inadequacies below. You must reflect deeply upon these, to appreciate the benefit of the Ichi school.

<u>OTHER SCHOOLS USING EXTRA LONG SWORDS</u>

Particular schools are very much focused on the use of extra-long swords, without consideration of cutting the enemy by any means necessary. This allows for a weak point in their training. They believe that with extra length they will defeat an enemy from afar.

In combat, reach advantage is certainly beneficial, but those that consider this alone definitely do not know strategy. This demonstrates the weak spirit of those men that rely upon the length of their weapon without really understanding strategy.

It cannot be the inevitable case that we lose for holding a short sword and not carrying with us an extra-long sword.

Once the distance has been closed, it becomes an encumbrance to wield this extra-long sword and it becomes inferior to a man's accompanying short sword.

I do not believe in disliking any weapon or technique in strategy, but what I do dislike is the inclination to one weapon only. A long sword does not necessarily beat a short sword, and likewise there are many cased of a small group of men overcoming many.

Your extra-long sword is of no use in confined spaces, for example a house.

Some men just do not have the same strength as others, and cannot overcome this strength purely because they hold an extra-long sword.

A narrow spirit is to be detested. Study this well.

THE STRONG LONG SWORD SPIRIT IN OTHER SCHOOLS

There is no strong nor weak sword.

You can wield a weak sword with a strong spirit and your cutting becomes solid. Likewise, you can wield a strong sword with a weak spirit and your cutting becomes dull.

There is no need to be concerned with the strength of the sword, giving too much thought to this will cause you to adjust your spirit in compensation. During one-on-one combat do not give thought to the strength of the sword nor your own, the focus must be to cut and kill the enemy.

Relying on strength alone will cause miscalculations when striking, and if you hit too hard you may cause your own sword to break. The saying 'the strongest hand wins' has no relevance here.

In larger scale warfare, if your army is strong, but enemy's is also, the combat will be brutal. The correct strategy must be used, otherwise there will be no winning. My school teaches to win through the wisdom of strategy, paying no attention to trivialities. Study this well.

USE OF THE SHORTER SWORD IN OTHER SCHOOLS

The use of a shorter sword is not the way to win in strategy. Historically, the long sword was called: tachi and the short sword was called: katana. For the strongest of men, the long sword is light, making the short sword unnecessary.

Some have the intention of leaping forward with the short sword, when the enemy's guard is down. This is a poor method to attempt to gain victory.

Aiming purely at a single unguarded moment is not the Way, this moment might not come, and what actions are performed while waiting? Additionally, this strategy will not work against multiple attackers. It is not possible to parry multiple swords with a short sword. This will lead to embarrassment and eventual death. This method bears no resemblance to the Way of strategy.

The way to win, is drive the enemy around with constant pressure. Make him squirm while you remain strong and firm.

This is the same strategy to be used in larger scale warfare. Overwhelm the enemy with large numbers and cause his swift end.

Most so-called strategists, are studying evading, counter-attacks and withdrawing. These then become their habits. There is one Way of strategy. Drive the enemy around with constant pressure, and make him obey your spirit.

OTHER SCHOOLS WITH MANY METHODS OF USING THE LONG SWORD

I think a misconception is taught in other schools, that there many methods of using the long sword. They do this to gain the esteem of beginners. They attempt to sell the Way. This is vile and repulsive.

To teach many Ways of cutting a man is a fallacy. Cutting the enemy is the Way of strategy, there is no use for many alterations of it.

Saying this, one must, according to the place, adjust you position so that your long sword will not be obstructed above or to the sides. You will need to hold the sword so that you can move it freely and unobstructed. There are five styles and five directions.

Anything beyond this is not the Way of strategy. Some teach, body bending, hand gesturing, jumping out and so on. To cut the enemy down, you must not twist or bend the body while making cuts. This is nonsense. In my strategy, the spirit and body are straight, upright, and cause the enemy to twist and bend. The winning spirit is to attack the enemy when his spirit is bent. Study this well.

USE OF ATTITUDES OF THE LONG SWORD IN OTHER SCHOOLS

Giving too much focus to particular styles, and attitudes is not the True way of strategy. To say this is how it has been done since ancient times or this is the modern way to do it, is also not the true Way.

There is one attitude that remains constant, and that is, maintaining an immovable spirit even during the most brutal assault. You must always hold the intention to take the lead and attack. You must appreciate this.

In combat, you must move the opponent's spirit. Aim for where his spirit appears weak, sow confusion, infuriate him, cause terror. When the enemy is disturbed, your moment to take full advantage has come.

I despise the defensive spirit, which these attitudes consist of. Therefore, in my Way of strategy, there is something called "Style-No Style".

An attacking spirit, is far different from a defensive one, and being attacked.

During combat, maintaining a strong spirit, parrying his movements, and subduing the enemy's attack, is like creating an impenetrable wall. When attacking, your spirit must drive deep in to the enemy, reinforcing his perception of your immovable spirit and this impenetrable wall. Study this well.

FIXING THE EYES IN OTHER SCHOOLS

It is maintained by some schools that your eyes should remain fixed in particular places, such as the hands, feet, or sword itself. However, by fixing your gaze upon these places, you will become disorderly and winning will slip from your grasp.

As an example, in team sports, you will not see sportsmen fix their eyes on the ball at all times, yet with experience they play very well and intuitively. By being accustomed to something, you are not narrowed to the use of your eyes only. Master musicians for example, play by ear, without reading the notes. Strategists can brandish the sword with ease, once they have mastered the Way, however to accomplish this, they do not fix their eyes on anything, or make random futile moves. It simply means they see naturally.

After many battles, you will come to effortlessly determine the enemy's speed, accuracy, position and spirit. The only fixed gaze in the Way of strategy is directly at the opponent's heart.

During larger scale warfare, the eyes must be open, not only to general sight, but to perception also. Perception in this scenario, means focusing on the enemy's spirit, discerning the terrain's condition, monitoring progress and any changes giving rise to favourable circumstances. This is the method for winning.

In one-on-one combat never fix the eyes on a particular detail. As mentioned before, if you fix your eyes on smaller details you will lose the larger picture, your spirit will become disorderly, and loss is inevitable. Research this and train well.

USE OF THE FEET IN OTHER SCHOOLS

Other schools make use of various foot techniques, which are completely unnecessary. They have names like: floating foot, jumping foot, and springing foot.

What a name to give the feet? Floating

foot! The Way must be walked firmly. Jumping foot! This is the sign of a jumpy spirit, when the spirit must be firm. Springing foot! The sign of indecision.

Depending on the terrain, these methods cannot be used. For example, soft marshy land is not a suitable platform for jumping from.

In my teachings, the feet are used the same as we do in day-to-day life, walking is walking. There is no need to lose control of your feet. The only adjustments to be made is found within the speed of movement and in adaptation to the enemy's spirit.

SPEED IN OTHER SCHOOLS

Speed is not a factor in the Way, and if we would like to use the word speed, the Master would appear slow.

In the Way of dance, talented performers can sing and dance at the same time, but if a beginner were to attempt this, their spirit would become slow and disorderly.

Fast melodies can be played so skilfully that they appear slow and tranquil. If a beginner were to attempt this, they would not be able to move fast enough for the melody to be calm. Only a highly skilled musician could move at speed and still remain slow. If you try to move hurriedly you will fall out of time. The skilful, are never out of rhythm and sync, they are always deliberate, but never appear in a hurry. This example highlights the principle.

The common conception of speed is of no use in the Way of strategy. Using this definition, in particular places, a marshy patch of land, or confined space for example, you would not be able to move quickly, or wield the sword at speed. Evaluate this.

When the opponent is rushing and reckless, you must remain calm and take advantage of the enemy's carelessness.

Do not let the opponent influence your spirit. With diligently training a calm spirit is yours.

"INTERIOR" AND "SURFACE" IN OTHER SCHOOLS

There is no "interior" nor "surface" in strategy.

Artistic achievements usually confirm inner understanding of secret teachings. In combat however, there no such thing as surface, or interior. When I teach the Way, training begins with techniques which are easy to understand for the pupil. Gradually there is an introduction to the deeper principles, and points which are hardly possible to comprehend initially, because the Way to understanding is through experience. This is why I do not teach surface and interior. I advocate experience.

If you decide to venture in to the mountains, and decide then to go deeper, and then deeper still, eventually you will emerge at the other side and the gate. Whatever Way you go, there is an interior, and a gate to it. However, in strategy, we are not able to say what is concealed by the gate, and what is revealed by entering. As such, I find difficulty in passing on my Way and teachings in writing.

Recognising the abilities of my students, I teach a direct Way, dispel bad methods of other schools, encourage action, and gradually introduce them to the true Way of the warrior.

I have tried to outline the strategies of other schools above, I could now list this schools one by one, but I have omitted their names intentionally.

The reason for this is that the methods pointed out above are collectively distributed between them, and that each school has various factions and refinements of the above.

If we look at them collectively, broadly and honestly, we see that they make use of long swords and short swords, and have much concern around strength in small scale battles and larger scale war. You by now will understand why I do not recommend going through the gates of other schools.

My school of the long sword consists

of neither a gate or interior. You simply must keep a clean and true spirit to realise the virtue of strategy.

Twelfth day of the fifth month, the second year of Shoho (1645) Teruo Magonojo SHINMEN MUSASHI

THE VOID BOOK

The Ichi Way of strategy is recorded in this the Book of the Void.

Nothing, this is the void. Man does not 'know' the void. Void is nothingness. By knowing tings in existence, we can know what is not in existence. This is the void.

Void, is not something that is misunderstood, this is incomprehension, and not the true void.

Warriors on the path, studying the Way of strategy sometimes make the mistake of thinking that which they do not know is the void. This again is not the true void.

The Way of strategy as a warrior is attained by studying all martial arts, but not straying from the true Way of the warrior.

With a calm spirit, accumulate time spent practicing, each day and as many hours as possible. Attend to the spirit, heart and mind, and hone the sight, perception and gaze. When the clouds of confusion clear, when the spirit is calm and relaxed, this is when there is a true void.

Without understanding the true Way, in which ever field of study, or in general common sense, you may feel as if everything is in order, and exact. However, when observing objectively, with a view taken alongside the universal laws of life, we find various doctrines which digress from the true Way.

With truth as the foundation on which to develop the true spirit of the Way. Carry out strategy directly, accurately and broadly.

By doing so, you will then find your view has become wider, and take the void as your Way, and the Way as your void.

Virtue is found in the void, no evil. Wisdom has continual existence, principles are forever, the Way can be found, spirit is emptiness.

Twelfth day of the fifth month, second year of Shoho (1645) Teruo Magonojo
SHINMEN MUSASHI

END

For more adapted classics by James Harris
please visit:

Http://ViewAuthor.at/JamesHarris